MARY HOFFMAN is the internationally acclaimed author of more than 100 books for children, ranging from picture books to teenage fiction. Her first picture book for Frances Lincoln, *Amazing Grace*, has become a classic which, with its sequels in the series, has sold 1.5 million copies worldwide. Mary's other picture books for Frances Lincoln include *The Colour of Home* with Karin Littlewood and *An Angel Just Like Me* with Cornelius van Wright, as well as the hugely successful *The Great Big Book of Families*, *The Great Big Book of Feelings*, *The Great Big Green Book* and *Welcome to the Family*, all with Ros Asquith. Mary Hoffman lives in Oxfordshire.

For more information about her books visit her website:
www.maryhoffman.co.uk

ROS ASQUITH has been a Guardian cartoonist for 20 years and has written and illustrated more than 70 books for children and teenagers. As well as *The Great Big Book of Families*, *The Great Big Book of Feelings*, *The Great Big Green Book* and *Welcome to the Family* with Mary Hoffman and *Max the Champion* with Sean Stockdale and Alexandra Strick, Ros wrote and illustrated the picture book *It's Not Fairy* for Frances Lincoln Children's Books. She is also the author of the *Teenage Worrier* series and *Letters from an Alien Schoolboy*, shortlisted for the Roald Dahl Funny Prize. Ros Asquith lives in north London.

For more information about her books visit her website:
www.rosasquith.co.uk

PEMBROKE BRANCH TEL. 6689575

For the Dell family: Andy, Sylvia,
Alastair, Kathryn, Olivia and Georgie,
who made a new family – M.H.

For Jessie, Lola, Lenny and Lucie Lorne – R.A.

JANETTA OTTER-BARRY BOOKS

Text copyright © Mary Hoffman 2010
Illustrations copyright © Ros Asquith 2010

First published in Great Britain in 2010 by
Frances Lincoln Children's Books,
74-77 White Lion Street, London N1 9PF
www.franceslincoln.com

This paperback edition first published in Great Britain in 2015

A CIP catalogue record for this book is available from the British Library.

ISBN: 978-1-84780-587-4

Illustrated with watercolours

Printed in China

1 3 5 7 9 8 6 4 2

The Great Big Book of Families

Where am I? Can you find me every time you turn a page? And can you find out my name?

Mary Hoffman

Illustrated by Ros Asquith

F

FRANCES LINCOLN
CHILDREN'S BOOKS

Once upon a time most families in books looked like this –

One daddy,   one mummy,   one little boy,   one little girl,

But in real life, families come in all sorts of shapes and sizes.

one dog   and one cat.

In this book are a lot of families living
in different ways. Perhaps there's one
that looks like yours?

FAMiLiES

Lots of children live with their mummy and daddy,

but lots of others live
with just their daddy

or just their mummy.

Some live with their grandma and grandpa.

The Great
Big Book
of Families

Some children have two mummies or two daddies.

And some are adopted
or fostered.

WHO'S iN YOUR FAMiLY?

Some people have lots of brothers and sisters...

and uncles and aunties...

and cousins...

and grandmas and grandpas.
And even great grandmas
and great grandpas.

Love from
Cousin Ed
Cousin Aisha
Cousin Sally
Cousin Hussein
Cousin Gavin
Cousin Leo
Cousin Lola
Cousin Jessie
in Kenny
in Fred
in Lara

But some people have really
small families. You can be a
family with just two people.

Dad
Me
MY FAMILY

HOMES

People live in all sorts of homes...

Some small families live in big houses.
And some big families live in tiny flats.

And some people can't find
anywhere to live.

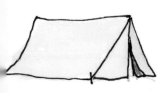

 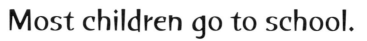

SCHOOL

Most children go to school.

But some are
taught at home.

And some just won't go to school.

But I've <u>been</u> to school already. I went <u>YESTERDAY</u>

Others are too young to go to school.

JOBS

GRAIN

In some families everyone has a job.

In others only one person goes out to work.

CEMENT

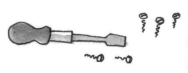

Some parents work from home.

And some can't get
a job at all.

HOLiDAYS

Some families go on exotic holidays,

and some stay closer to home.

Some visit families in other countries.

You don't need to pack EVERYTHING

And others go on day trips.

Not all families
can afford a holiday.
But most people
get some time off
from work. Even a
weekend at home
can be a little holiday.

FOOD

Some mums or dads are great cooks...

Others prefer to buy ready-made meals.

Most families get their food
from shops or markets.

But some people grow their own.

CLOTHES

Some children get new clothes.

Others have hand-me-downs...

Or their clothes come from charity shops.

Some families dress up for special occasions.

But some like to wear
jeans all the time.

And some dress any
way they please.

PETS

Some people believe their pets are members of their family.

And some pets think they're very important family members.

Some people even look like their pets.

Is a teddy a pet?

Some families can't have pets - but it doesn't stop them dreaming...

And there are ways that every family can have a pet of some sort.

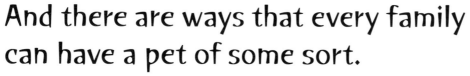

Am I a pet?

SNAIL RACE

CELEBRATIONS

Birthdays are fun, but some families make more fuss about them than others.

And then there is Christmas, Divali, Eid,
Hanukkah, Weddings, Christenings,
Bar and Bat Mitzvahs...
Chinese New Year...

Whatever you celebrate in your family,
there are usually some special traditions.

HOBBIES

In some families everyone has the same hobby.

In others, everyone likes doing different things...

TRANSPORT

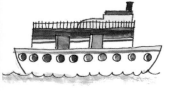

Some families walk everywhere –
to the shops, to school,
to the doctor...

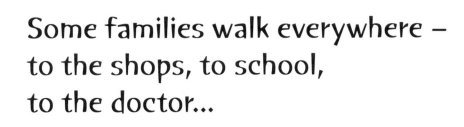

CARRY!

Others get about in big cars,

or on bicycles...

Or riding something else...

FEELINGS

In some families everyone shares their feelings.

Other people are more shy. Or perhaps they just like to keep their feelings to themselves.

Sometimes not everyone in the family feels the same way about things.

And feelings can change quickly.

Have you ever tried to make a family tree?

Sometimes you don't have to go back far to find bits of family who have come from other countries.

And if your mum or dad lives with a new partner,

you might have to make a whole new set of branches.

So families can be big, small, happy, sad, rich, poor, loud, quiet, cross, good-tempered, worried or happy-go-lucky.

Most families are all of these
things some of the time.

What's yours like
today?

MORE TITLES IN THE FANTASTIC GREAT BIG BOOKS SERIES:

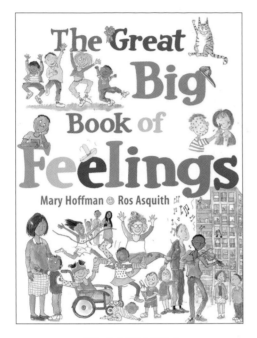

978-1-84780-281-1

THE GREAT BIG BOOK OF FEELINGS

How do you feel today? Happy? Sad? Jealous? Excited? Silly?
Or a mixture of all these and more…? Explore lots of different
feelings, and see if you can find feelings that match your own or
that help you understand how other people are feeling. And look
out for the cat on every page. He has feelings too!

"A terrific book – essential for schools and perfect for families"
– *Marilyn Brocklehurst, Bookseller's Children's Choice*
starred reviews from *Kirkus, Booklist, School Library Journal*

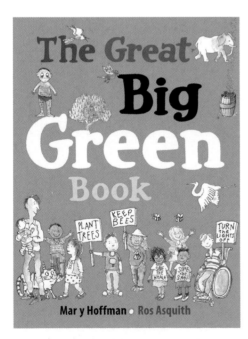

978-1-84780-445-7

THE GREAT BIG GREEN BOOK

Save water, save energy, recycle, ask questions – and help protect
the forests, oceans, fresh water and wildlife on our planet. With
clear information about life on Earth and important conservation
issues, accompanied by witty and wonderful illustrations, *The
Great Big Green Book* is packed with ideas and inspiration for ways
to keep our planet safe and beautiful for future generations of
children.

Frances Lincoln titles are available from all good bookshops.
You can also buy books and find out more about your favourite titles,
authors and illustrators on our website: www.franceslincoln.com